# ORGANIC GARDENING

## A Guide for Beginners

*by*

**Ruth Jacobs**

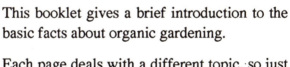

This booklet gives a brief introduction to the basic facts about organic gardening.

Each page deals with a different topic, so just look up the subject that interests you.

For further information, a selection of books is listed on page 47.

Copyright © Ruth Jacobs

**ISBN** 1 873727 07 0

**British Library Cataloguing in Publication Data.** A catalogue record for this book is available from the British Library.

**All Rights Reserved.** No part of this publication may be reproduced, stored in a retrieval system, or transmitted in any form or by any means, electronic, mechanical, photocopying, recording or otherwise, without prior written permission.

First published in March 1996 by *Alfresco Books*
7 Pineways, Appleton, Warrington, Cheshire, WA4 5EJ
*Telephone:* 01925 267503

**Publisher's Note:** While every effort has been made to ensure that the information given in this book is correct the Publishers do not accept responsibility for any inaccuracy.

**Cover** - Gordon Firth

**Line drawings** - Jackie Woolsey

**Typeset and design** - Jen Darling

**Production** - Coveropen Ltd

# CONTENTS

*Part 1:* **WHY ORGANIC?**                                *Page*

| | |
|---|---|
| Some common questions answered. | 6 |
| What is organic gardening? | 7 |
| What's wrong with artificial fertilisers? | 8 |
| Pesticides can damage your health. | 9 |
| Pesticides and the environment. | 10 |

*Part 2:* **ESSENTIAL BASIC KNOWLEDGE**

| | |
|---|---|
| What is soil? | 12 |
| What lives in the soil? | 13 |
| How plants feed naturally. | 4 |
| Mineral requirements | 15 |
| Minerals for Life | 16 |

*Part 3:* **CREATING A FERTILE SOIL**

| | |
|---|---|
| Organic matter is best. | 18 |
| Compost heaps | 19 |
| Leaf mould | 20 |
| Worm compost | 21 |
| Organic fertilisers | 22 |
| Comfrey in the organic garden | 23 |
| Green manures | 24 |
| More sources of fertility | 25 |
| Summary of organic fertilisers | 26 |
| Maintaining fertility | 27 |
| Crop rotation | 28 |

Page

## *Part 4:* FIGHTING PESTS AND DISEASES

| | |
|---|---|
| The story of insects | 30 |
| The first line of defence | 31 |
| Encouraging predators | 32 |
| Pest barriers | 33 |
| The slug problem | 34 |
| You've got a problem? | 35 |
| Mineral deficiencies | 36 |
| What's locked up? | 37 |
| Organic sprays | 38 |
| Some home-made remedies | 39 |
| Weed control | 40 |

## *Part 5:* SUMMING UP

| | |
|---|---|
| Getting started | 42 |
| Comparing pest and disease controls | 43 |
| Comparing feeding methods | 44 |
| Organic organisations | 45 |
| Organic supplies | 46 |
| Further reading | 47 |
| About the Author | 48 |

# Part One

# WHY ORGANIC?

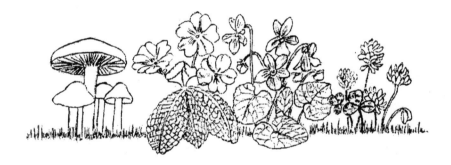

# SOME COMMON QUESTIONS ANSWERED?

Q   Does organic gardening mean just not using chemicals?
A   That's only the tip of the iceberg; there's a lot more to it.

Q   What does the word organic mean?
A   Anything that has been alive, either animal or vegetable. If it is mineral it is not (biologically) organic.

Q   Does that mean that organic gardeners never use minerals?
A   No. Organic gardeners *do* use some minerals as well but only naturally occurring ones.

Q   So why do they call it organic gardening?
A   It *is* confusing. A better name would be biological gardening.

Q   Why are organic vegetables better?
A   Organically grown plants are stronger and more disease-resistant; they contain more vitamins and minerals and don't absorb heavy metals from polluted soil in the same way that chemically grown plants do.

Q   Surely it's all right to use chemical fertilisers as long as we also use some organic material?
A   Page 8 explains the arguments against.

Q   Why do people use chemicals if organic methods are better?
A   The chemical industry spends vast sums on advertising; no-one advertises manure!

Q   How do you manage pests and diseases without chemicals?
A   By understanding a plant's needs and its enemies' habits.

**The following pages should help towards this understanding.**

# WHAT IS ORGANIC GARDENING?

- Organic growing means using no artificial fertilisers or chemical pesticides - it's a wholefood system. Only organic materials plus natural minerals are used.

- This way of growing respects the environment and is non-polluting. Modern methods destroy the natural world.

- Traditional gardening methods are combined with the most up-to-date techniques.

- It is also called biological or ecological gardening because only natural processes of recycling are used.

- It means feeding the soil, not the plant. Nature has designed plants to find their own food; they do it much better than we can.

- Organic growing is sustainable growing - a system that works indefinitely with a minimum of outside aid.

- It is vitally important to work with nature, not against. Nature ALWAYS wins any confrontation, as we know to our cost - ozone damage, poisoned seas, acid rain and the rest.

- Never forget that the soil is alive and that life must be cherished and preserved. This is the basic principle of organic growing.

- Preserving the balance of nature is an integral part of an organic system. We NEED the natural world: insects, flowers and wildlife.

- Organic gardening is conservation gardening.

# WHAT'S WRONG WITH ARTIFICIAL FERTILISERS?

- Feeding plants pure chemicals is unnatural; it is force-feeding, intensive care. Organic growing uses only natural substances.

- As chemicals are not a wholefood, the plant is deprived of many minerals and other substances needed for full health.

- Adding pure minerals causes an imbalance in the soil, making some elements unavailable to the plant: for example, too much potash deprives the plant of magnesium.

- Anyone eating such plants, either animal or human, could suffer from mineral deficiency. It is well known that the modern diet is lacking in essential minerals.

- Organic matter helps to filter heavy metals from the soil; plants chemically-fed will absorb cadmium rather than zinc, for instance.

- Chemical fertilisers encourage surface rooting at the expense of deep roots, making the plant susceptible to drought, floods and bad weather conditions.

- Chemicals usually mean overfeeding, leading to soft sappy growth which is mainly water and attracts pests.

- The surplus nitrates pollute drinking water and kill fish.

- Chemical fertilisers discourage the living organisms in the soil, sometimes killing them.

- Chemical fertilisers contain no humus, an essential component of soil. Without humus the soil slowly dies.

- Chemical farming is responsible for droughts in many parts of the world and for the USA dustbowl, where nothing grows.

# PESTICIDES CAN DAMAGE YOUR HEALTH

- These include fungicides, herbicides, weed killers, insecticides; all are biocides (life killers).

- Many are man-made inventions, similar to plastic or nylon and, like them, never rot down. They are here for good, in the air we breathe and the water we drink.

- Pesticide residues are in all our food and some of them are suspected of causing cancer, birth defects or genetic mutations, and other serious health problems over the long term.

- In the short term, handling chemicals may be even more dangerous; chemicals absorbed through the skin or inhaled can be lethal.

- So, they are a health hazard, both in the short and long term.

- Every year one or two are withdrawn from use, finally admitted to be dangerous. Which ones will be next?

- All the various chemicals combine to form a lethal, chemical cocktail, the effect of which is as yet unknown.

- They are passed down to babies in mothers' milk.

- Some biocides banned in the West are still being exported to the Third World, where thousands of people who handle them are poisoned every year.

- Much imported food contains British-made pesticide residues. So, despite the ban, we're still getting them!

- Do not be fobbed off with talk of 'insignificant amounts'. Our bodies are able to respond to minute quantities and an alien substance is still an intruder, no matter how small, and especially when taken regularly.

## PESTICIDES AND THE ENVIRONMENT

- Pesticides kill not only the pest but its enemies too. Pests are much more resilient - result - a pest population explosion.

- In time pests develop resistance to chemicals, so that more powerful pesticides have to be developed. The malaria mosquito, for instance, is now resistant to almost every known chemical.

- Some newer pesticides are aimed specifically at one pest, or are advertised as 'safer' because they deactivate in the soil, but their residues are just as deadly and long lasting.

- Farm weedkillers have killed 95% of English wild flowers. These so-called weeds are vital to provide habitats for friendly predators.

- As wild plants die, so does wildlife. A nesting pair of blue tits needs 15,000 caterpillars to rear a brood of young birds. No host plants? No blue tits.

- Poisoned insects and slugs are eaten by hedgehogs and other creatures. So poisons travel up the food chain, killing all the way. This nearly lost us all our golden eagles.

- Pesticides are polluting rivers and streams.

- They are present in all animals, including humans, and DDT is even present in Antarctic penguins.

- Sprayers are not accurately calibrated, so that droplets are floating in the air and being inhaled by us all.

- Pesticides interfere with the balance of nature, which normally prevents any one creature from becoming a nuisance. This is why slugs are such a problem; civilisation has removed many of their natural enemies.

- Pesticides kill not only the living creatures in the soil but the soil itself. If the soil dies, nothing will grow.

*Part Two*

# ESSENTIAL BASIC KNOWLEDGE

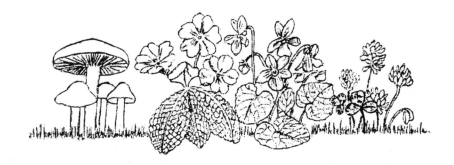

## WHAT IS SOIL?

- Plants will only thrive if the soil is healthy, so it's important to know something about the soil.

- Soil is the most important part of the garden: it has taken hundreds of years to build it up from the remains of plants, animals and ground-up rocks.

- Fertile soil containing plenty of organic matter is said to be in good heart, with a complete range of minerals, vitamins, proteins and other substances needed for plant health, as well as ample humus.

- A teaspoonful of soil contains literally millions of bacteria and fungi - micro-organisms, which need humus to stay alive.

- The only source of humus is organic matter, for example manure and compost, so regular applications are essential. There is no artificial or chemical substitute.

- Humus gives the soil structure, providing aeration and drainage, preventing waterlogging and anchoring the plants firmly.

- If no organic matter is added to the soil it slowly deteriorates and dies, becoming dry dust that blows or washes away - soil erosion.

- Once the soil is dead, nothing will grow in it, unless fed artificially.

- Peat, and its substitutes, are used in order to provide humus - a very inferior substitute for the real thing.

## WHAT LIVES IN THE SOIL?

- Healthy soil is teeming with life - insects, worms, slugs, plus millions of micro-organisms - bacteria and fungi.

- They all play a part in recycling organic material into food for the next generation of plants.

- Possibly the most important are the bacteria and fungi, all of which do a different job.

- Some bacteria work the nitrogen cycle, whereby they convert atmospheric nitrogen into nitrates, the basic plant food.

- Others decompose dead organic matter back again into free-floating nitrogen.

- Yet other microbes help to feed the plant, in a mysterious process in which the plant roots signal that food is needed.

- This is a typical example of the interdependence of all living things, plant and animal. We all need each other.

- The plant cannot obtain food unless it has the co-operation of these organisms, which is why nothing will grow in dead soil. Try sowing seeds after a bonfire!

- Bacterial activity is dependent on the soil being warm enough and having the correct acid/alkali balance.

- Because bacteria can't work in the cold, organic plants sometimes take longer to get started, but they soon catch up.

- Earthworms play a vital part in keeping the soil healthy; their tunnels loosen and aerate the soil; they improve the structure and help to produce humus. Healthy soil will contain lots of worms.

## HOW PLANTS FEED NATURALLY

- We don't need to feed plants; they feed themselves.
- But we do need to understand how they obtain their food.
- Plants feed in two ways - through their leaves and their roots.
- The leaves use carbon dioxide from the air to make growth, giving out oxygen in its place. This is called photosynthesis.
- This only happens in the light. Without light a plant dies.
- Plants also need minerals and other substances, usually taking them up through their lower roots.
- The plant selects which mineral it wants and only takes the amount it needs, when it needs it.
- Organic minerals, unlike the chemical sort, remain in the soil until needed, releasing their goodness very slowly so that over-feeding or imbalance is rare.
- Shallow surface roots are used by the plant to absorb water. Any chemical fertilisers added to the soil will dissolve into this water.
- In this way chemical fertilisers are absorbed by the plant immediately, causing a massive imbalance of minerals, while any surplus is leached away through the soil.
- Plants can also absorb some minerals through their leaves, either from the air or from a liquid feed.
- On the next page you will find details of the minerals and elements that the plant needs.

## MINERAL REQUIREMENTS

- Plants need a number of minerals, all of which are present naturally in fertile, organic soil.

- The most important minerals are nitrates, phosphates and potash, commonly known by their chemical symbols N, P, K.

- Nitrates (or nitrogen) feed the green, leafy part of the plant; phosphates (or phosphorus) build up the root system; potash (or potassium) contributes to fruit and flower development.

- Three other elements are needed in smaller quantities - calcium, magnesium and sulphur.

- Then there are the trace elements which are needed in tiny amounts; the main ones are boron, manganese, iron, copper, zinc and molybdenum, plus several others.

- A shortage of any of these may lead to serious deficiency, disease or even the death of the plant.

- On the other hand, the plant may show no symptoms at all, but the animals and humans eating them could suffer as a result.

- Chemical fertilisers usually contain only a very limited range of minerals, so that the plants often lack very important elements.

- It is now realised that today's modern diet is seriously deficient in minerals, such as zinc and magnesium, which are essential for the healthy development of both the nervous system and the brain.

## MINERALS FOR LIFE

- All plants - flowers, fruit and vegetables - need these minerals to keep them healthy.

**FLOWERS and FRUIT**

*Potash please!*

**LEAVES**

*I need nitrates!*

**ROOTS**

*Please feed me phosphates!*

# Part Three

# CREATING A FERTILE SOIL

## ORGANIC MATTER IS BEST

- Remember, organic gardeners feed the soil, not the plant, so it is important to give the soil plenty of organic matter - anything that has been alive and has rotted down.

- The best complete plant food is well-rotted manure or compost.

- If the manure has been mixed with wood shavings, don't dig it in but use it instead as a mulch around trees and shrubs.

- Pigeon and poultry manure are very strong and should be put in the compost heap. Avoid manure from battery units; it can be toxic.

- Use a green manure when possible. (See page 24.)

- Sewage sludge is sometimes available but, as a precaution, use only on non-food plants.

- Leaf mould is an excellent source of humus, containing a little plant nutrient. (See page 20.)

- Seaweed is a whole food, complete with humus. If you live near the sea, pile it round your vegetables. But seaweed is very susceptible to radioactivity, so check first.

- Spent mushroom compost is good but nowadays can be a highly chemical, synthetic substance; so make sure it is organic.

- Worm compost is very rich and easily made, or it can be bought. It is best used as a mulch or in potting compost. (See page 21.)

- Excellent organic commercial preparations are now available.

- No need to dig - just spread the material thickly over the soil.

## COMPOST HEAPS

- Any good gardening book will tell you how to make a compost heap, but there are one or two points to remember.

- A compost heap simply uses natural processes, speeded up.

- You can use almost anything that has been alive, including hay and straw, bracken, tea leaves, household waste, weeds and lawn mowings, old woollens, feathers, woollen carpets, hair, eggshells, rhubarb leaves, paper.

- You can safely use up to 10% newspaper, soaked and shredded.

- Avoid wood, tree leaves, man-made materials, metals, roots of perennial weeds, diseased plants, cooked food and meat. The last two encourage rats.

- Make sure your woollens and carpets *are* wool and not synthetic, as these will never rot down.

- If you can add a variety of weeds and wild flowers, your compost will be richer in vitamins and minerals.

- Animal manures added to compost are thought to convey extra disease resistance.

- An activator is not necessary if you have any soft greens such as lawn mowings, weeds or comfrey. Other activators are urine diluted with three parts of water and any manure, pigeon manure being the finest.

- The heap should get hot enough to kill weed seeds and most diseases. Use a good insulating material such as wood or brick and keep it covered - a carpet is fine.

- Always site your heap directly onto the soil so that earthworms can complete the composting process.

# LEAF MOULD

- Rotted-down leaves produce a peat-like substance known as leaf mould, traditionally used as a growing medium.

- Unaccountably, it has been neglected in recent years since peat has been available commercially.

- Simply collect leaves each Autumn and put them somewhere to rot down. A netting 'cage', or plastic bags, will keep them together.

- They don't need an activator, heat or air, just a little moisture. Press them down and leave.

- After a year they will have decomposed sufficiently to use as a mulch around trees and shrubs.

- In two years they will produce a superb, friable compost that is in every way a substitute for peat.

- It is very suitable for seed and potting compost when sieved. Being free from disease or weed seeds no sterilising is needed.

- This means that you have the advantage of live compost, which gives the plants a head start.

- Leaf mould contains only a small amount of plant food but is a rich source of humus. Earthworms will take it down to enrich the soil.

- Avoid using leaves from main roads; they may be covered with lead dust.

- Its greatest asset is that it is a renewable resource - no landscape has been destroyed to obtain it.

- And it's free!

# WORM COMPOST

- This system converts kitchen scraps and garden waste into a rich compost, ideal for a small garden or even no garden.

- The worms used are not earthworms but red brandlings used by fishermen. They can be found under damp surfaces in the garden or bought at angling shops.

- Any container can be used but an ordinary plastic dustbin with a well-fitting lid is quite suitable.

- Drill a few drainage holes about 15 cms from the base of the bin.

- Fill the bin with sand to a depth of about 20 cms and water this well. Cover with cardboard or wood cut to shape.

- On top of this comes the bedding - a few inches of peat substitute, leaf mould or old potting compost, for instance.

- Your bin is now ready to receive the worms, about 100 of which should be placed on the bedding. A layer of waste is now added.

- You can use almost anything organic - much more so than in a normal compost heap - meat, fish, bread, cooked food.

- As the worms slowly work their way through this material, keep adding further layers.

- The compost is ready in a few weeks and the worms and eggs go to start the new batch.

- Worm compost is too rich to use neat but makes nutritious mulch or a component of potting compost.

- Fuller details are available in an HDRA leaflet. (See page 46.)

# ORGANIC FERTILISERS

- There are several organic fertilisers available for those times when an extra mineral feed is needed.

- However, these are not pure chemicals but natural compounds which just happen to be rich in one particular mineral.

- They don't feed the plant immediately but decompose only slowly, releasing the minerals when needed.

- **Nitrates**: Dried blood is quick acting, although not now used by organic farmers because it is too soluble. Hoof and horn takes a few weeks to break down.

- **Phosphates**: Rock phosphate is a ground-up, natural rock. Bone meal is a renewable resource.

- **Potash**: Rock potash is a natural rock. Comfrey liquid or leaves are a renewable resource.

- **Calcium**: Ground limestone has a slower release than lime. Dolomite is approximately half calcium and half magnesium. Calcified seaweed is renewable and an excellent soil conditioner, with a wide range of trace elements but no nitrates.

- **All-round fertilisers**: Seaweed meal is one of the best. Apply three months in advance and lightly rake in.

- **General fertilisers**: Blood, fish and bone - but may contain chemical potash; or 3 parts dried blood, 6 parts bone meal and 8 parts seaweed meal; apply 110-170 grams per square metre.

- Some of the above are only obtainable from organic suppliers. (See page 46.)

## COMFREY IN THE ORGANIC GARDEN

- Comfrey, a perennial herb, is invaluable for the organic gardener.
- It is rich in all nutrients, especially potash. To use the leaves, cut down to 5 cms, with at least three cuts a year.
- Make a high potash fertiliser by putting the leaves in a container weighed down with a brick and leaving for 3 to 4 weeks. Dilute the resulting black liquid with about 20 parts of water.
- The leaves can also be used as a nutritious mulch around the base of the plants, breaking down rapidly.
- Placed thickly in the potato trench it will produce superb results. Leave 24 hours before planting to let the leaves wilt.
- Regular spraying with comfrey liquid improves a crop's health.
- It makes a good seed or potting compost, using half comfrey and half peat substitute, then left to rot down over the Winter.
- Comfrey is easily grown, its only disease being rust which can be cured by applying wood ash.
- Feed it with manure every Spring, preferably pigeon manure, obtainable free from pigeon fanciers.
- The roots go down very deep; so once planted it's hard to remove.
- It is easily propagated by means of root cuttings or offsets. Plant 60 cms apart.
- Comfrey is also a food, drink, animal fodder and medicinal plant.

# GREEN MANURES

- A green manure is a plant grown purely to improve the soil, a method used traditionally by farmers.

- Any ground that is temporarily unused will soon be covered with weeds, so it's better to grow a plant of your own choosing.

- In Winter, a green manure prevents nutrients being washed out of bare soil and protects it against harsh weather conditions.

- When you need the ground again, lightly dig the plants in. Allow about a week for them to decompose - longer if sowing seeds.

- At the young, sappy stage the decomposing plants will enrich the soil with minerals and humus. So don't leave them to get tough and woody.

- If legumes are chosen, your soil will benefit from the additional nitrate. (See page 27.)

- Some green manures, such as phacelia or buckwheat, have attractive flowers which are a magnet for friendly insects.

- Green manures must be chosen with care to suit the needs of a particular growing scheme. They may be composed of either annuals or perennials.

- Some will be killed by the first frosts, so saving labour, while perennials like alfalfa can be over-wintered, providing several cuts for the compost heap.

- The commonest plants used as a green manure include grazing rye, trefoil, winter tares, mustard and clover.

- Fuller details can be found in an HDRA leaflet.

## MORE SOURCES OF FERTILITY

- Nothing is ever wasted in the organic garden: almost everything organic can be recycled in some way.

- Wood ash from a bonfire is a good source of soluble potash; young twigs produce the most potash.

- Feathers are a very rich source of long-term nitrogen. Just tip them into a foot-deep trench and cover them with 20 cms of soil. This is ideal for all soft fruit but too rich for brassicas.

- Human hair, obtainable from the hairdresser, is also a useful source of long-term nitrogen.

- Tea leaves should never be thrown away. They contain slow-release nitrogen and the roses will appreciate them, as well as indoor plants. Cold tea contains potash.

- Soot is an old-fashioned fertiliser containing a little nitrogen, which helps to warm the soil and deter slugs.

- Nettles make a good liquid fertiliser. Soak in water and use the liquid.

- Any organic mulch will improve the soil. Shredded waste such as prunings, bark, sawdust, pine needles and bracken are all suitable.

- Foliar feeds are helpful when a plant needs a tonic. Use comfrey liquid or seaweed extract and spray the leaves.

A thick organic mulch with cold tea.
Just what your plants need.

# SUMMARY OF ORGANIC FERTILISERS

| MINERALS | FERTILISERS | OTHER SOURCES |
|---|---|---|
| **NITRATES** | Dried blood, hoof and horn. | Nettles, fish meal, soot, feathers, tea leaves, urine, legumes. |
| **PHOSPHATE** | Rock phosphate, bone meal. | Leaf mould, fish meal. |
| **POTASH** | Rock potash, comfrey. | Wood ash, nettles, cold tea, leaf mould, urine, young bracken. |
| **CALCIUM** | Ground limestone, calcified seaweed, dolomite. | Gypsum. |
| **MAGNESIUM** | Dolomite | Epsom salts (to correct deficiency only) |
| **BORON** | Borax (to correct deficiency only) | |
| **TRACE ELEMENTS** | Calcified seaweed, seaweed meal, liquid seaweed, comfrey. | |

## MAINTAINING FERTILITY

- Once you have achieved a really rich, fertile soil you must keep it like this to satisfy hungry plants.

- Regular applications of manure or compost are, of course, the main ingredient.

- Crop rotation is extremely important, giving the ground time to recover from each crop's action. (See next page.)

- All plants of the legume family (peas and beans) have bacteria in their roots which manufacture their own nitrates from the air.

- This is why organic farmers don't need to buy nitrates - they grow legumes such as clover and plough them in.

- When peas and beans have been harvested leave the roots and a short stem. The extra nitrate will enrich the soil.

- Grow a green manure in the Winter, on temporarily spare ground, and dig it in while young and sappy. This prevents nutrients washing away and feeds the soil. (See page 24.)

- Nature always covers bare soil quickly, so using green manures means adopting nature's ideas and improving on them.

- Avoid walking on the soil as plants cannot grow in compacted earth. It is a good idea to make permanent pathways in your vegetable plot; this saves compost too.

- Raised beds mean extra fertility and better texture; plants can be grown much closer together, with higher yields.

- Mulching with organic materials raises fertility and improves soil structure as the worms get busy; so use any of the materials mentioned on page 18.

## CROP ROTATION

- Never grow the same crops continuously on the same ground, to prevent exhaustion of minerals and to allow the soil to recover.

- Root crops feed heavily on phosphates; brassicas are greedy for nitrates; peas need extra potash. Moving them round spreads the load.

- A four-year rotation, as shown below, is good, but pick one that suits you. You may prefer the onion family, for example, rather than one of the others.

- The plant families are moved round clockwise each year, fitting in other crops where space is available.

- When planning your rotation, remember the following points:

    Brassicas (cabbage family) can suffer from clubroot, so wait at least four years before returning them to the same ground.

    Lime the brassica bed the Autumn before planting to deter clubroot.

    Potatoes must not have lime as this encourages scab.

    Let leafy vegetables follow legumes to take advantage of extra nitrogen.

    Never use fresh manure on root crops.

    Potatoes are the grossest feeders and usually have any compost or manure if only a limited amount is available.

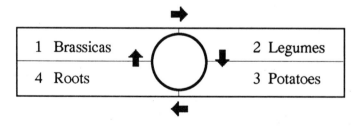

# Part Four

# FIGHTING PESTS AND DISEASES

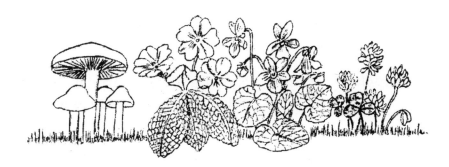

# THE STORY OF INSECTS

- Know your enemy - and your friends.
- Insects go through four distinct stages, varying in length according to weather conditions.

**Adult**

The adult insect usually lays its eggs on one particular plant family only, seeking it by sight and scent. It needs nectar to live.

**Eggs**

Look for eggs on underside of leaf and crush them before they can hatch.

**Caterpillar**

Caterpillar (grub, larva) spends its time feeding. This is when most damage is done. Remove by hand if possible. Caterpillars provide food for many predators, including wasps and birds.

**Pupa**

Pupa (chrysalis) lies dormant in soil or bark until conditions are right, when it sheds its skin and emerges as an adult. Birds and beetles eat most of them.

# THE FIRST LINE OF DEFENCE

- Prevention is always best, and most organic methods are ways of preventing the pest from reaching the plant.

- A healthy plant can resist attack; enemies always go for the weakest.

- There is no need for wholesale extermination of all insect life, just control. We can spare a leaf or two!

- Choose plants that are resistant to their particular disease: for instance, potatoes which are resistant to eelworm and roses which are resistant to blackspot.

- Grow the plant in the kind of situation it enjoys: for example, a shade-loving plant will not thrive in full sun.

- Move the plants round the plot. (See page 28.) Crop rotation prevents a build-up of soil pests.

- Encourage predators - the natural enemies of the pest and the gardener's friends. (See next page.)

- Use physical barriers to prevent the fly from reaching your plant. (See page 33.)

- Timing sometimes helps; sow carrot seeds when the carrot fly is laying her eggs, late May/early June or late July/early August.

- Avoid monoculture; cottage gardeners always grew their cabbages amongst the flowers to confuse the pests.

- Many people use companion planting; some plants thrive when grown together. Strong-smelling herbs planted in the vegetable plot can fool flying pests.

- Garden hygiene is important. Remove all decayed leaves and destroy diseased materials.

## ENCOURAGING PREDATORS

- A flock of birds on the lawn, ladybirds, beetles and other wildlife in the garden, are all busy accounting for millions of pests daily. We CANNOT do without them so don't kill them with chemicals.

- The most important thing you can do to encourage predators is to banish all chemicals, providing a safe environment.

- Organic pest control, in fact, depends on a good balance of both pests and predators.

- Make room somewhere for a few weeds, in other words wild flowers. These will provide a habitat for many predators as well as a home for friendly, pest-eating insects.

- Build a pond - a small one will do - and bring in frogspawn and toadspawn. Frogs and toads eat vast quantities of unfriendly insects and slugs.

- Encourage hedgehogs; these will dispose of many pests.

- Grow the kind of plants that attract hoverflies, such as marigold and poached egg plant. Hoverfly larvae account for many aphids.

- Birds are greedy for insects in all their stages, so attract them with bird boxes and tables, and grow berried plants. Seed heads left on plants throughout the winter are an important source of food at a difficult time of year for birds.

- Hang pieces of fat in apple and rose trees. Birds will come for the fat and take caterpillars and pupae while there.

- A flock of free range hens pecking round fruit trees will dispose of codling moth and other unwanted pupae.

- The best slug remover, undoubtedly, is a couple of ducks.

## PEST BARRIERS

- Barriers of different kinds are ideal to keep out the flying pest that is looking for somewhere to lay her eggs. Once the grub is hatched, the problem is much more difficult.

- Probably the best barrier is netting of the correct mesh size, ranging from very fine spun nylon mesh against carrot fly to a fruit cage against birds.

- A square of underfelt around the plant is very efficient in keeping out cabbage root fly. It also has the advantage of harbouring beetles, one of the most useful predators in the garden.

- An upturned yoghurt carton with a hole burnt in the base, put firmly round young plants, keeps out root flies, cabbage moth and the cutworm.

- A polythene or fine mesh 'wall' round the carrot bed, about 60 cms high, deters carrot fly. The barrier's warming effect is a bonus.

- Sprinkle gritty material around plants to deter slugs. (See next page.)

- Sections of plastic bottles pressed in around vulnerable plants will keep out slugs and some other soil-borne pests.

- Study the habits of pests and devise your own barriers and deterrents!

## THE SLUG PROBLEM

- Undoubtedly, this is the most widespread problem in the garden, although slugs are useful scavengers.

- Slug pellets can damage or kill wildlife and pets.

- The best long term solution is to encourage predators but ducks are the most efficient. (See page 32.)

- Certain precautions will help, the main one being to keep the ground clean and free of decaying leaves, a slug's staple diet.

- However, some people believe that a mulch of mowings and decaying leaves keeps the slug happy and away from precious plants, but this will increase the slug population.

- Slugs dislike anything rough on their slimy bodies. So sprinkle grit, ashes, shredded bark, egg shells, soot or similar material round vulnerable plants. Some will need renewing after rain.

- A popular remedy is to sink a jar of weak beer in the soil at ground level. Slugs are attracted to this and drown. Unfortunately, so do friendly beetles. If this happens raise the level of the jar.

- One idea is a miniature electric 'fence' around the bed, which is a good idea as long as no slugs are within the enclosed area.

- The most effective protection of young plants is a section of plastic bottle pushed firmly into the ground around each plant, which also acts as a miniature greenhouse.

- Many people go slug-hunting at night with a torch; hundreds can be caught in this way. Pick them up with tweezers and drop them into a bowl of salty water. Alternatively, put damp newspapers on the ground and periodically remove slugs which collect underneath.

- A biological control now available is proving quite successful.

## YOU'VE GOT A PROBLEM?

- Despite all our efforts, there will still be some pests and diseases or the plants may not be developing correctly. So first find the cause of the trouble.

- Check that your cultivation techniques are correct for that plant: for instance sprouts like firm ground. And is the plant happy in its allotted position?

- You may have sown the seed too early before the soil has warmed, or it may have rotted or been eaten by mice. Every seed requires a different germination temperature.

- Constant inspection of plants will help to catch problems before they have a chance to become disasters.

- Remove pests by hand if possible. Look on the underside of leaves for eggs and caterpillars.

- Many apparent diseases are really signs of mineral deficiency. (See next page.)

- If your soil is deficient in one mineral, find out why. Has it been locked in by a too-generous application of some other mineral? (See page 37.)

- If you are unsure how to cure it, spray the leaves with liquid seaweed. This contains every mineral and the plant will take what it needs.

- Many tricks and traps exist for individual problems. (See the catalogues of organic organisations on page 45.)

- Observe good garden hygiene; remove dead leaves and branches, particularly if diseased.

- If all else fails use a spray but **only** an organic one. (See page 38.)

## MINERAL DEFICIENCIES

Always look up the symptoms of mineral deficiency first before assuming that your plants have some terrible disease. Here are some of the commonest symptoms ...

| Mineral Deficiency | Symptom | Short-term Cure | Long-term Cure |
|---|---|---|---|
| **Nitrate** | Pale, under-sized, poorly developed leaves. | Dried blood, hoof and horn. | Organic matter |
| **Potash** | Brown on the outer leaf edge, chocolate spot on broad beans. | Comfrey liquid or wood ash. | Rock Potash |
| **Phosphate** | Purple or blue-green tints on leaves. | Comfrey liquid or liquid seaweed spray. | Bone meal or rock phosphate |
| **Magnesium** | Yellowing leaves but veins stay green. | 28 grams Epsom salts in 9 litres water, over 2 square metres, or as foliar feed. | Dolomite |
| **Boron** | Brown curd in cauliflower, brown rot in swedes. | 1 teaspoon borax in 4.5 litres water over 6 square metres. | Calcified seaweed, seaweed meal. |
| **Calcium** | Blossom end rot in tomatoes. | Lime | Dolomite or calcified seaweed. |

If you're not sure of the correct cure, spray with liquid seaweed.

# WHAT'S LOCKED UP?

- It is extremely important that minerals are present in the soil in the right proportions to each other. If there is too much of one kind, others may become locked up and unobtainable. Too much trace element is as bad as too little.

- For this reason, approach soil testing with caution. There may be plenty of minerals in the soil but the plant cannot get at them.

- For example:

| an overdose of: | leads to locking up of: |
|---|---|
| potash | boron and magnesium |
| lime (calcium) | boron, iron, manganese |
| nitrate | calcium and copper |
| magnesium | calcium |
| phosphate | zinc and potash |

- Plants fed organically rarely suffer from locking up deficiencies or overdoses, because minerals in organic matter are present, naturally, in the right proportions.

# ORGANIC SPRAYS

- Organic pesticides, made from either vegetable or animal substances, break down quickly in the soil, doing no lasting harm.

- Nevertheless, these sprays do kill insects, so use them only as a last resort and as late as possible in the evening when friendly insects have retired for the night.

- The best all-round spray is soft soap, which is effective for aphids and small caterpillars. Add it to other sprays as a wetting agent.

- Derris is very effective for many pests but kills beneficial insects, so use it sparingly. It breaks down in 48 hours.

- Pyrethrum is equally effective for many pests but breaks down in 12 hours.

- The best caterpillar spray is BT, which is a bacterium that is specific to caterpillars only. Several other biological controls are now becoming available.

- Burgundy and Bordeaux mixtures are fungicides which are permitted where no other remedy is available. Research is continuing to find a more environmentally-friendly fungicide.

- Quassia chips are excellent for sawfly.

- There are now several other commercial preparations which are safely organic, one of which is insecticidal soap.

- Many of these sprays can only be obtained from suppliers of organic materials. (See page 46.)

- **NB** Some organic sprays may contravene new regulations, so check first: for example, nicotine, the traditional remedy for sawfly, has been withdrawn from the market because of legislation.

## SOME HOME-MADE REMEDIES

> The following traditional remedies can no longer be recommended because of EC legislation.

- The liquid from boiled-up rhubarb leaves makes an excellent aphid killer. Simmer 40 grams leaves in 1 litre water for $1/4$ hour, diluting with 3 parts water.

- Elder leaves boiled up similarly are equally effective and are also a mild fungicide, giving some protection against blackspot.

- Urine can be sprayed on fruit trees and is effective against scab - sprayed neat in January and diluted 3 to 1 before leaf fall.

- To eliminate ants, which protect aphids, mix equal parts icing sugar and borax; then sprinkle the mixture in their usual haunts.

- Bicarbonate of soda is quite an effective, mild fungicide for powdery mildew. Mix 2 teaspoons to 4.5 litres of water, add a little soft soap and spray twice a week.

- People used to boil up a brew of strong smelling herbs such as tansy or garlic, spraying it as a masking scent against flying pests.

- A pot of French marigolds in the greenhouse usually deters whitefly.

- Tagetes minuta has root secretions that can kill ground elder, bindweed and eelworm.

- Continued research is turning up new remedies and ideas for defeating pests and diseases. Yet old-fashioned ones still have their uses: for instance, permanganate of potash and washing soda were both popular at one time as fungicides.

# WEED CONTROL

- There is no organic weedkiller but some weeds, which are only wild flowers, should be given some space somewhere in the garden to provide a habitat for friendly insects and other predators.

- Constant hoeing will prevent weeds getting a hold while plants are becoming established.

- Remember that plants can't live without light, so a light-proof mulch will prevent weeds from growing.

- Suitable materials are black polythene, cardboard, carpet or several thicknesses of newspaper. They can be disguised with chippings or shredded bark.

- Regular organic mulches will suppress annual weeds while feeding the soil.

- A way of cleaning the vegetable plot before sowing is to allow annual weeds to germinate on the seedbed first, removing them before sowing.

- Some people use a flame gun to burn weeds on path or plot. This is very effective but must be used with care.

- Discourage perennial weeds by constantly removing leaves and flowers. In a couple of years, they will give up.

- To get rid of perennial weeds in the lawn, an old pair of scissors or a knife will remove the root.

- Boiling water is very effective for spot-weeding.

- Perennial weeds in the flower bed can be removed by covering thickly with a loose organic material, so that the roots grow into it and can, in time, be easily lifted.

*Part Five*

# SUMMING UP

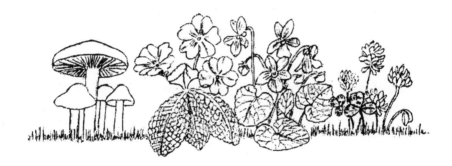

## GETTING STARTED

- You've decided to go organic but don't know where to start?

- First, put all your chemicals in the bin, then start a compost heap.

- Get some manure; riding schools and farms often sell it cheaply.

- Use only well-rotted manure and make sure it's mixed with straw and not wood shavings.

- If you have no manure or compost, apply a general fertiliser. (See page 22.)

- Try to manage two applications of organic matter, one in Autumn, another in Spring. Apply it thickly to the soil's surface.

- If your soil is still impoverished or acid, calcified seaweed will perk it up.

- Don't expect your vegetables to be fully organic for two or three years if you have previously used chemicals. They will only gradually leach away.

- Grow attractant flowers near the vegetables to attract bees, hoverflies and other beneficial insects. Herbs are a good idea too.

- You may get very poor results for a year or so until a proper balance has been established, but be patient and persevere. You won't regret it.

## PEST AND DISEASE CONTROL
## A Comparison of Different Methods

| CHEMICAL | ORGANIC |
|---|---|
| Chemical sprays poison and kill the soil. | Sprays are harmless and enrich the soil. |
| Most pesticides kill all insects indiscriminately. | A wide variety of insects are encouraged. |
| Herbicides destroy wild flowers. | Wild flowers are an essential part of organic growing. |
| Handling pesticides endangers human health. | No danger, only healthy activity. |
| Residues in food cause ill health. | Organic food is good for you. |
| Chemicals fight and confront nature. | Organic methods respect and promote the natural world. |
| Biocides endanger the food chain. | All creatures proliferate in safety. |
| The balance of nature is destroyed. | The balance of nature is an integral part of pest control. |
| The whole environment is polluted - air, land and water. | It conserves and improves the environment. |
| Chemicals are expensive to buy. | Many organic methods involve no cost at all except physical effort. |

**Are you creating an environmentally hazardous zone?**

# FEEDING THE PLANT
## A Comparison of Different Methods

| CHEMICAL | ORGANIC |
| --- | --- |
| Immediate take-up by plant. | Slow release - only taken up when required. |
| Usually causes overdose of nitrates. | Plant takes the amount it needs and no more. |
| Often deficient in trace elements. | Supplies full range of minerals and trace elements. |
| Interferes with and upsets natural processes. | Reinforces nature's bio-system. |
| Earthworms either killed or deterred. | Earthworms multiply rapidly in this favourable habitat. |
| Uses up the earth's supply of non-renewable resources. | As few renewables used as possible. |
| Encourages shallow rooting. | Leads to deep roots and good healthy root system. |
| Slowly destroys the humus. | Develops and maintains humus. |
| Toxic minerals easily absorbed. | Mainly filters out harmful elements. |
| Pollutes water, encourages algae. | Conserves the natural environment. |
| Very expensive to buy. | Many materials are free and involve recycling what would otherwise be garbage. |

# ORGANIC ORGANISATIONS

**Henry Doubleday Research Association,**
National Centre for Organic Gardening,
Ryton-on-Dunsmore, Coventry, CV8 3LG
*Telephone:* 01203 303517

**Soil Association,**
86 Colston Street, Bristol, BS1 5BB
*Telephone:* 01272 290661

**WWOOF** (Working Weekends on Organic Farms),
19 Bradford Road, Lewes, E. Sussex, BN7 1RB

**Biodynamic Agricultural Association,**
Woodman Lane, Clent, Stourbridge, West Midlands, DY9 9PX
*Telephone:* 01562 884933

**Good Gardeners' Association,**
Two Mile Lane, Gloucester, GL2 8DW
*Telephone:* 01452 305814

**Centre for Alternative Technology,**
Machynlleth, Powys, SY20 9AZ
*Telephone:* 01654 702400

## ORGANIC SUPPLIERS

**Henry Doubleday Research Association,**
National Centre for Organic Gardening,
Ryton-on-Dunsmore, Coventry, CV8 3LG
*Telephone:* 01203 303517
*Seeds, gardening products, books, food and gifts. (Personal customers only.)*

**Soil Association,**
86 Colston Street, Bristol, BS1 5BB
*Telephone:* 01272 290661
*Books and gifts.*

**Simpsons Seeds,**
27 Meadowbrook, Old Oxted, Surrey, RH8 9LT
*Telephone:* 01883 715242
*Untreated seeds and gardening products.*

**Chase Organics (GB) Ltd,**
Coombelands House, Coombelands Lane, Addlestone, Weybridge, KT15 1HY
*Telephone:* 01932 820958
*Seeds, gardening products and books.*

# FURTHER READING

*Organic Gardening* by L D Hills

*A Month by Month Guide to Organic Gardening* by L D Hills

*Companion Planting - Successful Gardening the Organic Way* by Gertrude Franck

*RHS Organic Gardening* by Pauline Pears and Sue Stickland

*The Complete Manual of Organic Gardening* edited by Basil Caplan

*Successful Organic Gardening* by Geoff Hamilton

*The Gardening from Which? Guide to Gardening Without Chemicals* by The Consumers Association

---

**The Henry Doubleday Research Association** has a large selection of books and pamphlets dealing with specific topics.

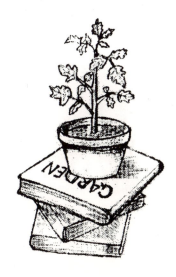

# ABOUT THE AUTHOR

- Ruth Jacobs, an organic gardener for over thirty years, is the co-founder and secretary of her local organic gardening group.

- This book has been written for the many puzzled gardeners Ruth meets who want to know more about organic growing. Based on the notes and handouts she used when lecturing for the WEA, it aims to answer some of the many queries she still receives.

- Ruth is on the writing team of the magazine, **Organic Gardening** - an essential buy for all enthusiasts - and has appeared on TV's Channel 4 in the *All Muck and Magic* series.

- Ruth lives with her husband on the outskirts of Liverpool, where her garden abounds with wild flowers, herbs, vegetables and fruit - all organically grown, of course!